Find Your Voice: Lead Your Life

Find Your Voice: Lead Your Life

Dr. Regina Banks-Hall

RBH Professional Publishing

Copyright © 2025 by Dr. Regina Banks-Hall

All rights reserved. No part of this publication may be reproduced, distributed, or transmitted in any form or by any means, including photocopying, recording, or other electronic or mechanical methods, without the prior written permission of the publisher, except in the case of brief quotations embodied in critical reviews and certain other noncommercial uses permitted by copyright law.

For more information contact:

Dr. Regina Banks-Hall, regina@rbhprofessionaldevelopment.com or by phone at 866-600-6322

Book design by: RBH Professional Publishing a division of RBH Professional Development Institute

ISBN Paperback: 979-8-9893303-6-2

ISBN Hardcover: 979-8-9893303-4-8

eISBN: 979-9-893303-7-9

DEDICATION

This book was written to encourage everyone to find their own voice, so they can take control of their life. This book is for those, who believe their voice does not matter. This book is dedicated to my husband Dolphus Hall, Jr. who continues to encourage me to inspire others and use my gifts. Thanks for all your support.

Contents

Introduction		1
1.	The Catalyst for Change: My Journey Into Leadership	5
2.	Clarity In Identity	9
3.	Breaking Barriers to Authenticity	15
4.	The 3 C's of Courageous Communication	21
5.	Boundaries Without Burnout	25
6.	Steps to Success: Power Phrases for Leaders	31
7.	The Power of Story: Leveraging Your Narrative as a Leader	37
8.	Leadership Across Domains	41
9.	Finding Your Voice: A Pathway to Resilience	45
10.	Emotional Intelligence: The Heart of Effective Leadership	49
11.	Daily Habits of a Voice-Driven Leader	53
12.	Crafting Your Personal Vision Statement: From Voice to Vision	59
13.	Mentoring: Teach Others How to Lead with Voice	65
14.	Mastering Your 30, 60, and 90 Day Action Plan	71
15.	The Importance of Finding Your Authentic Voice	77
16.	Measuring Growth: Indicators of Leadership Success	81

17. Resources for Growth	85
18. Key Insights for Impactful Leadership: Three Takaways to Remember	89
19. Conclusion	93
About the Author	97

Introduction

Discover Your Power Within

Welcome to Find Your Voice, Live Your Life! I'm Dr. Regina Banks-Hall, and I am thrilled to welcome you on this transformative journey through my latest book, Find Your Voice, Lead Your Life. If you're holding this book in your hands right now, you're already step one into a world designed to uplift and empower you—after all, finding your voice isn't just about speaking; it's about leading the life you deserve.

Let's take a moment to reflect on where you are right now. Perhaps you're a struggling business owner, an entrepreneur trying to carve out your niche, or a leader in your community who feels overshadowed by the chaos of daily challenges. Trust me, I understand your struggle—I've been there too. I know how it feels to be weighed down by self-doubt, to question your abilities, and to wonder if you are making the right choices. It can be easy to lose ourselves amidst the grind, to neglect our own needs while striving for success.

Through this book, I aim to help you reclaim your power. As a best-selling author, motivational speaker, trainer, and licensed coach, I have had the privilege of guiding countless individuals like you toward their true potential. My mission is to illuminate your path by helping you find your unique voice, which is key to leading and inspiring others around you.

In Find Your Voice, Lead Your Life, you will discover practical exercises, thought-provoking insights, and heartwarming anecdotes that illustrate the profound impact of self-discovery. Together, we will explore the potent connection between self-love and leadership. Each chapter will unveil strategies to break free from the chains of self-sabotage and negative thoughts that may have held you back for far too long. And, dear friends, I assure you: you have every right to succeed!

One of the most liberating aspects of this journey is realizing that you have the ability to define your own purpose. Throughout our time together in these pages, I'll guide you to articulate what truly drives you and how to harness that passion to impact those around you positively. Imagine waking up each day with a sense of clarity, ready to tackle challenges and lead by example. Sounds incredible, doesn't it?

But remember, this isn't just a theoretical exercise. I invite you to embrace each lesson actively and apply it to your life. The power to lead and create a fulfilling life rests within you. All it takes is the courage to recognize that your voice matters, not only for you but for the countless individuals who look to you for guidance and inspiration.

So, as you flip through the pages of Find Your Voice, Lead Your Life, don't just read—engage. Take notes, answer the reflection questions, and perhaps even jot down your thoughts and feelings in the margins. I want this book to be a living dialogue between us, a safe space for exploration and growth.

I encourage you now to take that first step. Set aside some quiet time today—maybe with a warm cup of tea—just you and your new book. Allow yourself to dive into this experience openly. I promise: your journey to empowerment and leadership begins now.

Thank you for joining me on this wonderful adventure. I can't wait to see how you will use your newfound voice to lead and inspire others, just as I believe you are destined to do. Let's turn the page together and embark on this incredible journey. Here's to finding your voice and leading your life with purpose and passion!

1

THE CATALYST FOR CHANGE: MY JOURNEY INTO LEADERSHIP

Have you ever had a moment that changed everything? A moment that felt like the ground had opened up beneath your feet, forcing you to reassess where you were headed? For me, that moment came in 2009, during a difficult time for many, the economic downturn. The economic downturn led to the sad news that I had been laid off. At first, I felt lost, like a ship drifting in a stormy sea without a compass. Days turned into weeks, and weeks turned into months of feeling sorry for myself. But, just like clouds parting to reveal a bright sun, I made a decision that would forever change my life.

I picked myself up. I dusted off the self-pity and decided it was time to focus on my future. I returned to school to pursue a Master's Degree, fueled by a fire to learn and grow. I would continue my education and earn a doctoral degree in Leadership. I was beginning a new journey.

At the same time, I stepped in to help my family when my father-in-law fell ill. This unexpected responsibility changed my perspective. I found myself spending hours in a nursing home, and it was there, in that rather somber environment, where I discovered a whole new calling.

As I sat in the nursing home, observing the daily routines, I noticed something troubling. The nursing assistants who took such great care of the patients were for the most part unhappy. They complained about their jobs, expressing frustration and dissatisfaction. It broke my heart to see these dedicated individuals feeling so powerless, like they were stuck in a dark tunnel with no way out. But in that moment, something incredible happened. I felt a spark of inspiration.

I decided to take action. While sitting there with my father-in-law, I began encouraging the nursing assistants. I shared stories of how I had also felt lost and unsure, but I found that taking charge of my own journey helped me immensely. I told them they had the power to change their own destiny—if they wanted to. It was not just talk; I truly believed in their potential. One by one, they began to listen. They began to believe.

With each conversation, I saw a change in their expressions. Their eyes lit up with new possibilities as they considered enrolling in nursing school. I saw courage blooming where before there had been doubt. When these talented individuals began to come back into the room filled with enthusiasm and excitement about taking that leap into nursing education, I was overwhelmed with joy. Their success became my success, and in that shared journey, I discovered something powerful: I was meant to coach others.

It was within those nursing home walls that the seeds of RBH Professional Development Institute were planted. I realized that helping others navigate their paths to success was where I wanted to direct my energy and focus. It wasn't just about leading people to a better career; it was about empowering them to embrace their own leadership journeys. This experience beautifully illustrated that everyone, regardless of their circumstances, has the power and potential to lead.

As I reflect on this period, it becomes clear to me that leadership is not reserved for those in top positions. It is in the spirit of encouragement, the small acts of kindness, and the relationships we build. It lies in recognizing that every individual has the ability to inspire change—not just for themselves, but for others in their lives. Like those nursing assistants who dared to dream, you too can take charge and transform your destiny.

So, dear reader, as you embark on your leadership journey, remember that you have the power within you. Each step you take, each choice you make, is a ripple that can lead to greater waves of change. Leadership is not a title; it's an action, a way of being. You don't have to wait for permission to lead—just like I didn't have to wait to encourage those nursing assistants. Start by believing in yourself and others will start believing in you too.

In this ever-changing world, embrace your leadership potential. Whether you're an unemployed worker searching for your next opportunity, a business owner trying to revive your company, or an aspiring investor looking for guidance, know that you have the capability to forge your own path. Your experiences, struggles, and triumphs can inspire others.

As you turn the pages of your own story, take a moment to discover what ignites your passion. The leadership journey is not a straight road; it's filled with twists and turns, challenges and celebrations. Yet, each moment can be a catalyst for greater things. Your journey can inspire those around you just like my journey did for those nursing assistants.

As you strive for your dreams, always remember: you can lead. You are a beacon of potential, capable of inspiring change in others. So take that first step, embrace the challenges, and know that you are indeed a catalyst for change. The world is waiting for your leadership to shine!

Chapter Summary

- Discover your power! Start believing you can change your own life today.

- Take action! Talk to others about their dreams and inspire them.

- Join a leadership program! Look for opportunities to learn leadership skills and grow.

- Reflect often! Think about how you can uplift others while pursuing your own path.

2

CLARITY IN IDENTITY

Have you ever sat quietly and asked yourself, "What is my purpose?" It's a big question, isn't it? In our fast-paced world, it's easy to get lost in the hustle and bustle of everyday life. We juggle jobs, family, and other responsibilities, often forgetting to check in with ourselves about what really matters. This chapter is all about helping you carve out your place in this world by finding your purpose and top values. So, take a deep breath, grab a comfy chair, and let's dive in!

Understanding Your Purpose

Your purpose is like a guiding star—it helps you navigate through life. For some, it might be making the world a better place, while for others, it could be supporting their family or creating amazing art. My purpose, for instance, is all about helping others discover their unique gifts. I do this through motivational speaking, coaching, and teaching. It's fulfilling and lights up my path every day!

But how do we actually find our purpose? First, think about what you love to do. What activities make you lose track of time? What topics get your heart racing? Reflecting on these questions can shine a light on your deep-rooted passion!

The Power of Values

Now that we have a sense of purpose, let's talk about values. Your values are like your personal road signs. They tell you which way to go and what's important to you. For example, if kindness is one of your values, you might find joy in volunteer work or simply helping a friend in need.

To really understand your values, try writing down a list of things that matter most to you. This could include family, honesty, adventure, creativity, or even learning. Once you have your list, narrow it down to your top three or four. These are the values that will accompany you on your journey to fulfillment!

Discovering Your Gifts

Finding your purpose also links closely to recognizing your gifts. What skills do you have that others admire? Perhaps you're an amazing listener or a fantastic problem-solver. By identifying and embracing these gifts, you become empowered to share them with the world.

Let's take a moment to think about some examples. Consider a girl in your class who's great at making people laugh. Her gift could lead her to become a comedian, teacher, or even a motivational speaker—just like me! Remember, everyone has something special to offer, and it's our job to discover and nurture those talents.

Aligning Purpose, Values, and Gifts

When you align your purpose, values, and gifts, magic happens! It's like being on a roller coaster that navigates through the most exhilarating twists and turns—but this time, you're riding it with confidence. For instance, if your purpose is to uplift others, your value of kindness will drive you, and your gift of oration will give you the voice to inspire change.

This alignment is crucial. When we know what we stand for and the talents we possess, making decisions becomes easier. Should I take that job where I'll feel unappreciated? Or should I choose to follow my heart and work in a field where I can help others? Clarity allows you to weigh your options with assurance.

The Importance of Clarity

"Clarity creates confidence," and this statement holds tremendous power. Imagine trying to drive a car at night with foggy headlights—it would be challenging, right? Similarly, when you lack clarity, navigating your life can feel daunting and confusing. You're left guessing about the right choices, leading to stress and uncertainty.

On the contrary, when you know your purpose and values, confidence becomes your co-pilot. You're equipped to face challenges and seize opportunities boldly. You can step out into the world, knowing who you are and what you stand for. That's a game-changer!

Getting Started on Your Journey

So, how can you start this exciting journey toward clarity? Begin by journaling! Write about your dreams, your passions, and the values that excite you. Consider seeking feedback from friends and family, too. They might see strengths in you that you hadn't noticed before.

Another great exercise is to visualize where you see yourself in the next five or ten years. What do you want to be doing? Who do you want to help? This vision can become a powerful fuel that propels you toward your purpose.

Surrounding Yourself with Support

In this journey of self-discovery, it's vital to surround yourself with supportive people. Seek out those who inspire you and lift you up. Join groups or community organizations that resonate with your values. Engaging with others who share your goals and ambitions can further illuminate your path. Remember, empowering voices create an environment where everyone flourishes!

The Impact of Clarity

As you strive for clarity in your identity, keep in mind that this isn't just about you. The clarity you gain can inspire those around you. When you live your purpose authentically, you shine a light for others—encouraging them to embark on their journeys of discovery as well.

Final Thoughts

Now that we've explored the connection between clarity, purpose, and values, I hope you feel inspired to take action. Remember that this journey isn't a sprint; it's a marathon. It takes time, reflection, and sometimes a little trial and error. But trust the process! With each step you take, you're solidifying your identity and building confidence.

So go ahead and keep asking yourself, "What is my purpose?" and "What are my top values?" Finding clarity in identity can truly set you free to live a fulfilling and impactful life. Embrace the adventure—you never know what exciting discoveries await you!

Chapter Summary:

- Take time to reflect on what makes you happy and passionate.

- Write down your top values to guide your life decisions.

- Identify your unique gifts and share them with the world.

- Seek support from inspiring people and communities around you.

3

BREAKING BARRIERS TO AUTHENTICITY

Have you ever felt like you had to put on a mask to fit in, whether at school, work, or even at home? You are not alone! A lot of people, including business owners, counselors, women leaders, and anyone wanting more out of life, grapple with this issue. This chapter is all about breaking barriers to authenticity, and we're going to tackle three sneaky villains: fear, imposter syndrome, and cultural conditioning. So, grab a snack and let's dive into how we can shake off those masks and discover our real selves.

Understanding Fear

Fear is one of the biggest roadblocks to being authentic. It can be scary to share your true thoughts or ideas because you might worry about what people will think. Picture this: you're in a meeting with your colleagues, and you have a brilliant idea, but then a little voice inside your head says, "What if they laugh at me?" Those worries can hold you back from speaking up. To kick fear to the curb, try this: when you feel that fear rising, breathe deep and remind yourself of the things you believe in. What's more important, your voice or someone else's judgment? By prioritizing your feelings, you'll feel more empowered to share your authentic self.

Imposter Syndrome: The Sneaky Thief

Now let's take a closer look at imposter syndrome. This is that thing where people feel like they're not really good enough to do what they do, even if everyone else thinks they're amazing! If you've ever thought, "I don't belong here," when you actually do, then you've experienced imposter syndrome. But guess what? It's all in your head! Start by writing down your accomplishments. Yes, I mean it! List everything from the smallest to the largest, and look at that list when those feelings creep in. Remember, everyone has moments of doubt, but recognizing your achievements can help you step into your power.

Cultural Conditioning: The Rule Book We Didn't Sign Up For

Cultural conditioning is another tricky barrier. We grow up learning certain beliefs about how we should act or what we should achieve. Maybe your family believes that success means a high-paying job, or perhaps your culture has specific expectations about roles. This conditioning can stifle your true voice. To break these chains, reflect on your values. Ask yourself: "What do I believe about success?" or "What truly makes me happy?" It's important to challenge these inherited beliefs and replace them with what feels right for you.

Finding Your Voice

Once we tackle fear, imposter syndrome, and cultural conditioning, the next step is discovering your authentic voice. Think about what makes you unique. It can be anything from your creative ideas to your way of solving problems. A great way to explore this is to try journaling. Write about who you are, what you're passionate about, and how you want to be seen in the world. This exercise can be tremendously revealing—it's like shining a flashlight on the hidden corners of your heart.

Embrace Vulnerability

Being authentic also means embracing vulnerability. It's okay to show your true emotions and admit when you're struggling. For example, if you're a leader in your company, sharing your challenges can actually build trust with your team. When you let your guard down, it encourages others to do the same. So, the next time you feel nervous sharing something personal, remember: Vulnerability isn't a weakness; it's a strength.

Speak Your Truth

Once you've discovered your authentic voice, it's time to shout it out! Literally! Practice speaking your truth in small settings—like with a friend or family member. Share your dreams, your worries, and your ideas. As you start to express yourself more, you will grow in confidence. Each time you do this, you peel away another layer of that mask you've been wearing.

Inspiring Others

Here's where it gets exciting! When you own your authentic voice, something magical happens: you inspire others. Imagine this scenario: you confidently share your story in a group, and someone else feels inspired to do the same. You're not just freeing yourself; you're liberating those around you, helping them find their voice too. It creates a beautiful ripple effect.

Connecting with Others

Finding your authentic voice also helps you connect with others on a deeper level. When people see that you're being real, they feel more comfortable opening up. It's a win-win situation! Whether you are in business meetings, workshops, or social gatherings, the connections you make will be meaningful and genuine. This authenticity can foster better teamwork and collaboration.

Overcoming Setbacks

Keep in mind that the journey to authenticity is not always smooth. You might face setbacks or feel the urge to fall back into old habits. That's okay! When these moments happen, remind yourself of your purpose. Reflect on that list of accomplishments again, and give yourself grace. Remember your journey is valid and every step you take is progress.

The Power of Community

Lastly, surround yourself with a supportive community. Join groups or networks where authenticity is valued. Engaging with others who share your struggles and aspirations encourages you to keep pushing through. Together, you can help each other break down barriers and celebrate your true selves.

Conclusion

So, there you have it—by confronting fear, imposter syndrome, and cultural conditioning, we can strip away our masks and embrace authenticity. Take a moment to recognize that owning your authentic voice doesn't just help you; it empowers those around you. When you let your true self shine, you liberate others to do the same. So, let's lift each other up and create an environment where everybody feels comfortable being who they truly are. In the end, we're all in this together on the journey to authenticity!

Chapter Summary:

- Confront your fears by prioritizing your voice over others' judgments—speak up!

- Write down your successes to combat imposter syndrome and recognize your worth.

- Challenge cultural beliefs by identifying your true values and defining your own success.

- Embrace vulnerability to build trust, inspire others, and create meaningful connections.

4

The 3 C's of Courageous Communication

Have you ever found yourself in a conversation where you just wanted to avoid talking about certain topics? Maybe it's a tough talk with a friend about their behavior, or a heart-to-heart with your boss about a project that's not going well. It's natural to steer clear of these sticky situations, but what if I told you that facing these conversations head-on is more important than you might think? In this chapter, we'll dig into the exciting world of what I like to call The 3 C's of Courageous Communication.

Let's start with the first "C": Courage. Now, you might be thinking, "Courage? Isn't that just for superheroes?" Well, not quite! Courage is not just for caped crusaders. It's a quality that each and every one of us possesses. It's about finding the strength to say what needs to be said, even when it feels a bit scary. Think about it this way—every time you take that leap of faith to open up, you are stepping into a new territory, one that might be intimidating but also very rewarding.

Moving on to the second "C": Compassion. This is where you care about how your message affects others. When we communicate with compassion, we consider the feelings and viewpoints of the people we're talking to. This is crucial because it helps us to connect with others on a deeper level. For instance, if you need to talk to a co-worker about missing deadlines, approaching them with kindness can change the entire tone of the conversation. Instead of coming off as critical, your compassion can turn that tough talk into a constructive discussion.

Now let's explore the third "C": Confidence. It's one thing to have courage and compassion, but if you lack confidence, your message might not land in the way you hope. Confidence means believing in yourself and the importance of your words. When you speak with confidence, others are more likely to listen. So, whether you're leading a team meeting or simply giving someone important feedback, showing that you believe in what you're saying is super key.

Now, using the 3 C's together is like creating a powerful recipe for success in conversation. Let's break it down with a real-life example! Imagine you're at work, and you notice a colleague who consistently undermines others' ideas in meetings. You feel you're avoiding the conversation because you're worried it might lead to conflict. However, remember the 3 C's! Approach this conversation with courage, show compassion for your colleague's perspective, and communicate it with confidence. You might just find that this person wasn't aware of how they were coming across.

But what happens if we choose to keep avoiding those tough conversations? Well, often, problems don't solve themselves. If left unattended, issues can grow larger and more complicated. It's like ignoring a small leak in your house; if you don't fix it, your entire home could suffer water damage! As business owners, leaders, and aspiring achievers, facing important conversations can keep our relationships and projects healthy and thriving.

Now, you may wonder how to really practice these 3 C's in your own daily life. My suggestion? Start small. Pick one conversation you've been putting off and ask yourself how you can incorporate courage, compassion, and confidence into that discussion. Maybe it's asking for help from a friend or offering constructive feedback to a colleague. The key is to take baby steps—every small win builds your confidence for the bigger ones!

In the end, remember this: speaking truth with care and conviction is not just a nice idea; it's essential for growth. When we speak plainly and kindly, not only do we elevate ourselves, but we also inspire others to take action. Courageous communication allows us to connect, share ideas, and resolve conflicts in ways that not only benefit ourselves but also enhance the communities we're a part of.

So, as you go about your day, I encourage you to reflect on the conversations you might be avoiding. Ask yourself: "What message am I holding back, and how can I communicate it courageously?" Embrace the 3 C's, and watch how your relationships and opportunities flourish.

Let's empower ourselves through courageous communication, so we can uncover our gifts and inspire others in the process. You've got this!

Chapter Summary:

- Face tough talks with courage to strengthen your relationships and resolve issues.

- Communicate with compassion to connect deeply and create a positive discussion.

- Show confidence in your words to ensure your message is heard and valued.

- Start small by tackling one hard conversation at a time, and build your skills!

5

BOUNDARIES WITHOUT BURNOUT

Where Am I?

Imagine you're running a race, and suddenly, you realize you've strayed a little too far from the track. You're off course, tangled in the bushes, and feeling frustrated. That's what happens when we lose sight of our boundaries—those invisible track lines that keep us focused and energized.

As business owners, entrepreneurs, counselors, and women leaders, you wear many hats. You're the motivator, the problem-solver, the dream chaser, and sometimes, the one working the late shift to help everyone else. The urge to help and inspire others is powerful, but don't forget: your purpose needs protection! *That's where boundaries come into play.*

Understanding Your Purpose

Your purpose isn't just a fancy motto to slap on your website. It's the heart of everything you do. When you focus on nurturing your gifts—whether it's motivational speaking or coaching—those gifts act like a beacon. They guide you and those around you toward success. But how do you maintain that energy and enthusiasm without burning out?

Establishing clear boundaries allows you to safeguard your purpose. Think of boundaries as a fence around a garden. It keeps out what could harm your plants while letting in the sunshine and rain they need to grow. If you don't define your boundaries, you risk having your garden trampled by the chaos that life can throw at you!

Recognizing the Importance of Boundaries

Let's break it down. Why are boundaries so super-duper important for leaders like you? Without them, your time and energy get eaten up. You may find yourself saying "yes" to every request, and before you know it, you're zapped of all your spark. Many people think that being a good leader means sacrificing your needs for the sake of others, but that's a recipe for burnout.

By setting clear limits, you not only protect your well-being but also illustrate to those around you that your time, energy, and talents are valuable. Models matter, right? Be the leader who shows that boundaries can coexist with compassion and collaboration.

Creating Your Connection

Have you ever tried to connect with someone but found that they're constantly distracted or overwhelmed? That's what happens when you don't have boundaries; your message gets lost in the noise. When you set those boundaries, you create space to be present with your team, clients, and community.

Now, how can you start drawing those lines? First, you need to know where your limits lie. Is your calendar filled to the brim? Are you skipping meals because you're too busy? These are signs that it's time to hit the brakes and assess what matters most.

How to Build Boundaries

Start by identifying what you're okay with and what you're not. Write this down! From working hours to personal time, making these boundaries explicit helps not just you but everyone in your circle. They'll understand when you're available and when you need to recharge.

Another tip? Communicate! Once you've established your boundaries, gently but firmly assert them. This isn't about being bossy; it's about being clear. Invite feedback, too. Sometimes, people may not realize they're crossing a line.

The Ripple Effect of Healthy Boundaries

When you define and enforce your boundaries, you inspire those around you to do the same. Imagine a workplace where everyone respects personal time and understands that productivity dips when we're running on empty. Wouldn't that be incredible? It creates a culture where everyone feels valued and energized to contribute.

And remember, boundaries aren't a sign of weakness; they're a form of self-respect. By respecting your own boundaries, you teach others to respect theirs. It's a beautiful cycle of encouragement!

Finding Balance: Work & Life

So, how do we balance work and life while keeping up with our purpose? It's not always easy, but setting aside specific times for work tasks versus "you" time is crucial. Turn off work notifications after hours, pick up that book you've been meaning to read, or take a walk in the park.

This balance isn't just a luxury; it's a necessity for mental health. You can't pour from an empty cup! When you take the time to recharge, you'll return to your work revitalized and excited.

Keep Checking In

Here's the secret sauce: regularly check in with yourself about your boundaries. Life changes, and so do we! What worked last month might not resonate with you now. Always listen to your gut feeling—it's an amazing guide when it comes to feeling stretched too thin.

Your purpose thrives when your energy is preserved. So ask yourself: Am I still on the right path? What do I need to adjust? Getting answers to these questions can illuminate the way forward while maintaining a healthy respect for your boundaries.

The Big Takeaway

In conclusion, remember this: *Boundaries preserve your energy.* They are not walls that keep you from connecting with others; instead, they're the fence that protects your beautiful garden of purpose. The more you respect and affirm your boundaries, the more you can inspire and uplift those around you.

So let's transform our approach! Make boundaries a part of your leadership strategy. You'll find that preserving your energy not only enhances your life, but it also boosts the lives of everyone you touch. You've got beautiful gifts to share—so let those boundaries shine!

Chapter Summary:

- Set clear boundaries to protect your purpose and avoid burnout.

- Communicate your limits openly to inspire others around you.

- Prioritize work-life balance with designated "you" time for self-care.

- Regularly reassess your boundaries to ensure they align with your needs.

6

STEPS TO SUCCESS: POWER PHRASES FOR LEADERS

Have you ever noticed how a few simple words can change everything? Think about it: the right phrase at the right time can lift you up when you're feeling down or inspire action when people are hesitant. In this chapter, we're diving into the power of phrases and how they can fuel your journey to success as a leader. So let's buckle up and explore how the right words can transform your leadership style!

Understanding Power Phrases

First, let's break down what we mean by "power phrases." These are words or expressions that can inspire, motivate, and clarify thoughts. Imagine you're trying to motivate your team on a tough day. A phrase like "Together, we can overcome any challenge" not only brings everyone together but also shines a light on the strength of teamwork. It creates a culture of collaboration and positivity that is essential for any leader.

The Power of Language in Leadership

Have you ever heard the saying, "Words create worlds"? It may sound a bit cheesy, but it's true! Leaders have a special responsibility to shape their environments with their words. When you speak with intention, you offer clarity and direction to your team, making them feel focused and empowered. In contrast, muddled communication can lead to confusion and frustration, which is the last thing any leader wants.

Building a Motivational Culture

Let's think about your workplace. When leaders use encouraging power phrases, they set the tone for a motivational culture. For example, if you say, "I believe in you," you're not just complimenting someone; you're building their confidence. People are more likely to take risks and be creative when they feel supported. That's the kind of culture every leader strives to create!

Examples of Power Phrases

Here are some specific examples of power phrases that can help you lead more effectively:

1. "Your ideas matter" – This phrase shows appreciation for your team's input.
2. "We're in this together" – This reaffirms the power of working as a unit.
3. "Let's learn from this" – Instead of focusing on failure, this encourages a growth mindset.
4. "Success starts with you" – This reminds individuals that their contributions are critical.

Using these phrases regularly can promote positivity and a sense of ownership among your team.

Finding Your Voice

Now that we understand the significance of power phrases, let's talk about finding your unique voice. Every leader has their own style, and it's crucial to express yourself authentically. You'll want to choose words that resonate with who you are. This authenticity builds trust, and when your team trusts you, they're more likely to follow your lead.

Knowing When to Use Power Phrases

Timing is everything! While power phrases are effective, using them at the right moment is just as essential. For instance, if your team is facing a tough deadline, saying, "We've faced challenges before and we can do it again!" can revitalize everyone's spirits. However, throwing out phrases haphazardly without context may just roll off people's backs.

Leading with Empathy

A great leader is also an empathetic one. It's important to read the room and adjust your language accordingly. If someone is having a tough day, a gentle, "I see that you're struggling, and that's okay. What can I do to help?" shows that you recognize their feelings. This type of communication fosters a supportive atmosphere and encourages openness, building stronger relationships.

The Ripple Effect of Your Words

The impact of your words doesn't stop with your immediate team. When you use power phrases, they create a ripple effect that extends beyond your office walls. Colleagues who hear positive interactions are likely to carry that same energy into their conversations, spreading a culture of encouragement throughout the organization. Like a pebble dropped in a pond, one encouraging phrase can create waves of positivity!

Words Can Build Confidence or Create Confusion

As we wrap up this chapter, remember that words hold power. They can either build confidence or create confusion. As a leader, it's your job to ensure clarity through your communication. A simple, "I trust your judgment" can boost someone's confidence immensely. On the flip side, vague language can leave people feeling uncertain and anxious.

Conclusion

So as you continue your journey in leadership, keep in mind the importance of choosing your words wisely. Embrace the power of phrases that inspire and uplift, and be intentional in your communication. Words can create an amazing culture and a thriving team environment. Remember: with great power comes great responsibility. Use your words to empower others, and watch as you inspire those around you to reach new heights!

Now get out there and start crafting your power phrases. Your journey to effective leadership starts with just a few words!

Chapter Summary:

- Communicate your limits openly to inspire others around you.

- Prioritize work-life balance with designated "you" time for self-care.

- Regularly reassess your boundaries to ensure they align with your needs.

7

THE POWER OF STORY: LEVERAGING YOUR NARRATIVE AS A LEADER

Have you ever listened to a really great story and felt like you were right there, experiencing everything along with the characters? That's the magic of storytelling! It connects us, inspires us, and helps us understand one another better. In the world of business and leadership, storytelling is not just a fun way to share ideas. It's one of the most powerful tools you can use to lead others and make a difference.

So, why is storytelling so impactful in leadership? First, stories connect vision to emotion. When you tell a story, you don't just share facts. You create a vivid picture that helps people feel something. For instance, think about a time when a product or service made someone's life better. When you share that story, you let your audience feel the joy, struggle, or hope tied to that experience. This emotional connection can motivate them to take action, whether that means joining your team, supporting your cause, or working harder towards a shared goal.

Let's explore how great leaders use storytelling. Imagine a coach who tells a story about a time their team faced a tough challenge but came together to win. Through this narrative, the coach not only shares valuable lessons but also instills a sense of unity and determination in the players. They remember that they are not just individual athletes; they are part of a team that can achieve greatness through collaboration and perseverance. This is the kind of powerful impact a well-told story can have.

Moreover, storytelling links strategy to people. In business, leaders often have big goals and plans. However, if they just present these strategies as dry data, people might feel confused or disconnected. But when leaders embed these strategies within personal narratives, it becomes relatable and easier to understand. For example, if a business owner shares a story about how customer feedback led to a new product and improved sales, employees can see how their contributions matter and how they can drive change together.

Now, let's talk about your personal narrative. Every leader has a unique story. It includes your successes, failures, and everything in between. The key is to share this story in a way that resonates with others. Think about your journey and the challenges you faced to get to where you are today. What lessons have you learned? How have they shaped your vision for the future? By sharing your experiences authentically, you create trust and inspire others to share their stories too.

For instance, let's say you started a small bakery from your kitchen. You faced countless sleepless nights perfecting your recipes and overcoming business hurdles. When you share your struggles and successes with your team, they see your passion and dedication. They become motivated to contribute to your bakery's growth because they understand where you're coming from, and they want to be part of that journey.

As a leader, you can also use storytelling to drive performance. Think of it as aligning your team's daily tasks with the bigger picture. Share stories of past successes that align with your current goals. For example, if your team is hesitant about a new project, tell them about a time when you faced doubt but persevered. Such stories can inspire confidence and can ignite a fire within your team to strive for the common vision.

When you craft your stories, consider incorporating various elements that can elevate the narrative. Show vulnerability—don't shy away from discussing failures or setbacks. Embracing your imperfections humanizes you and allows others to relate more deeply. Add humor and warmth to lighten the mood and engage your audience.

Additionally, use visuals where appropriate—think images, videos, or simple props. These can reinforce your stories and help audiences remember your message. If you're discussing a specific campaign, show them photos or data that illustrate the journey, making it not only an exciting tale but also a visual narrative.

Furthermore, storytelling isn't just about you; it can also be about your community or team. Celebrate the diverse stories within your organization to create an inclusive environment. Encourage your team to share their stories during meetings or through company newsletters. This not only builds camaraderie but also enriches the company culture, creating a richer tapestry of experiences that everyone can learn from.

The conclusion you want to draw from all this is simple yet powerful: Storytelling is a blueprint for inspiring others. It connects, motivates, and creates meaning. When you embrace your narrative and use it strategically, you can empower those around you to reach their full potential.

So, as you step into your role as a leader, remember the stories that shaped you, and realize the incredible impact they can have on others. Whether it's a quick anecdote during a meeting or a full-fledged presentation, use the power of storytelling to inspire your team. Let your narrative be a catalyst for action, transformation, and connection. With the right story, you have the ability to change hearts, minds, and even the course of your organization. So craft those stories and let them propel you forward as the leader you aspire to be!

Chapter Summary:

- Share your personal story to connect emotionally and inspire your team.

- Use storytelling to make your goals and strategies relatable and clear.

- Encourage team members to share their stories for a stronger community culture.

- Embrace vulnerability and visuals in your storytelling to engage and motivate others.

8

LEADERSHIP ACROSS DOMAINS

Leadership is one of those words that gets tossed around a lot. You might hear it in meetings, at school, or even in your living room when someone is trying to take charge of the TV remote! But have you ever stopped to think about what leadership really means? Leadership isn't just about giving orders or being the boss; it's about inspiring others, making connections, and consistently showing up as your best self in all areas of life—self, work, family, and community.

So, which leadership domain is the strongest, and which needs a little bit of work? It's a question many of us ponder, especially as we strive to be better leaders in our own lives and careers. The truth is, the strongest domain might depend on where you currently stand and where you want to go. But one thing is clear: each domain is interconnected and can uplift or drag down the others. When we focus on our strengths, we have the chance to inspire those around us and help them find their own gifts.

Let's start with the 'self' domain. This is all about personal growth. Leadership begins from within. Think about your passions, interests, and the skills that make you uniquely you. Do you enjoy solving problems? Are you great at motivating your friends? Understanding who you are and what you bring to the table is key. Once you know yourself, it's much easier to lead others. When you nurture your personal growth, you become a stronger leader—not just for yourself, but for those around you as well.

Next, we have the 'work' domain. This is where many people think leadership shines the brightest. In a workplace, your leadership style can really shape team dynamics. Are you the encouraging type who celebrates even the small wins? Or are you more of a taskmaster who focuses on results? Both styles can be effective, but consistency is crucial. When your teammates know what to expect from you, they're more likely to trust you and feel empowered to do their best work. But remember—what works in the office might not translate to your home life or community. You must find a balance.

The 'family' domain is another important area for leadership. In your family, leadership often requires patience, empathy, and understanding. Whether you're guiding children, supporting parents, or caring for siblings, your leadership helps shape the family environment. Perhaps you organize family game nights or listen patiently to someone's worries after a tough day. When you take the time to build relationships within your family, you're not just leading; you're creating a safe space for everyone to grow together.

Now let's talk about the 'community' domain. This is where your leadership can ripple out into the world. In your community, you can be a voice for change, a connector of people, and a source of inspiration. Whether you decide to volunteer, run for a local office, or simply help a neighbor, your actions can make a difference. Just like with family and work, your consistency in showing up for your community—whether big or small—will build your credibility as a leader.

But here's the kicker: the strongest leadership domain isn't black and white. It's not always easy to write down which one is best. Sometimes, personal growth is the freshest, but the family might need your focus, or your workplace could call for strong leadership. The real challenge is recognizing when to lean into one domain and when to balance them all.

Perhaps one way to bridge the gaps is through motivational speaking, coaching, and teaching. Sharing your story and listening to others can be incredibly empowering. When you inspire others to discover their own gifts, you encourage a community of leaders to flourish. It's like planting seeds: you nurture your own garden of leadership, and in turn, you help someone else grow their own.

As we explore these four domains, it's important to remember that leadership is about consistency. That's the secret sauce! When you show up as a true leader in every part of your life—whether you're at work, with family, or in the community—you build trust. People believe in you and want to follow your lead. With each consistent action, you lay another brick in the foundation of your credibility.

In conclusion, think of leadership as a balanced meal. You need some protein (self), vegetables (work), grains (family), and maybe a touch of dessert (community) to create a nourishing experience. The stronger you are in these areas, the more powerful your impact will be. So, whether you consider yourself more of a leader at home, work, or beyond, remember this: consistency builds credibility. By showing up consistently, you empower yourself and others to lead rich, fulfilling lives—together.

And that's what makes true leadership so powerful. It connects us, uplifts us, and inspires us to strive for more, not just for ourselves, but for everyone around us. So go ahead, embrace your leadership journey across all domains and watch the ripple effect of your actions transform lives!

Chapter Summary:

- Discover your strengths in each leadership domain for personal and community growth.

- Show up consistently at work, home, and in your community to build trust.

- Nurture relationships with family and friends to create a supportive environment.

- Inspire others through sharing your story and empowering their leadership journeys.

9

FINDING YOUR VOICE: A PATHWAY TO RESILIENCE

Have you ever felt like you had something important to say but didn't know how to say it? Maybe you felt shy, scared, or unsure of what would happen if you did share your thoughts and feelings. You're not alone! Every one of us has a unique voice that deserves to be heard, and finding that voice can help us build resilience in different areas of our lives. In this chapter, we'll explore how discovering and expressing your voice can be a powerful tool for overcoming challenges and becoming stronger than ever.

Let's start with figuring out what we mean by "voice." Your voice isn't just the sound that comes out when you speak; it's also your ideas, beliefs, feelings, and experiences. When you express these aspects of yourself, whether through speaking, writing, singing, or even art, you activate a force that can help you navigate tough situations. It's like having a superpower! And the best part? Everyone can tap into it!

One of the best ways to strengthen your voice is through self-expression exercises. These exercises can be fun and simple, like keeping a journal. Try writing down your thoughts every day. Don't worry about grammar or spelling; just let your ideas flow. This practice helps you connect with what's inside, boosting both your confidence and your resilience.

Here's a cool exercise to get started: write a letter to your past self. What would you want to say to that version of you? You can talk about the challenges you faced and share how you've grown since then. This exercise not only helps you find your voice, but it also reminds you of your strength. You've been through so much, and your voice has played a big role in your journey!

Next up, let's dive into vocal empowerment. This is a fancy term that means using your voice in a way that makes you feel strong and confident. You might wonder how to go about this, and that's okay! Here are some strategies: Start small by practicing speaking in front of a mirror, reciting affirmations or positive statements. See your reflection smile back at you as you say, "I am strong," or "I can handle whatever comes my way!" Over time, these affirmations will help you feel more resilient in the face of challenges.

Another great strategy for vocal empowerment is joining a local group or club that allows you to speak up and share your thoughts. Whether it's a book club, a debate team, or even a community theater, being part of a group gives you a chance to practice using your voice. Plus, you'll meet people who can cheer you on and provide encouragement, which can be a huge booster for your resilience!

Let's discuss adversity for a moment. Everyone faces challenges in life – that's just part of being human. But how we respond to those challenges can make all the difference. When you feel strong enough to voice your feelings, fears, and hopes, it enables you to tackle setbacks head-on. Think of your voice as a shield and a sword that armors you up!

Take a moment to think of someone you admire for their resilience. Maybe it's a famous person like Malala Yousafzai, who uses her voice to speak out for education, or someone in your life who has faced difficulties and come out stronger. Notice how their voice has helped them thrive despite adversity! You can draw inspiration from their stories and realize that you, too, have the power to rise above challenges with your voice.

Now, let's get practical again. Create a "Voice Empowerment Plan." Here's how you can do it:

1. **Set Goals**: Ask yourself what you want to express. Is it your dreams? Your opinions on a topic? Your feelings about a situation?

2. **Practice Regularly**: Whether it's journaling, speaking in front of friends, or singing – make it a habit to use your voice.

3. **Seek Feedback**: Talk to trusted friends or family members about your thoughts and feelings. Their feedback can help you see your progress and encourage you.

4. **Reflect and Adjust**: After practicing, take time to reflect on how it felt to express yourself. What worked? What didn't? This reflection helps you grow stronger.

As we wrap up this chapter, remember that embracing your voice is essential for developing resilience and overcoming challenges. Your voice is a gift, scattered within your heart and mind, waiting for you to share it with the world. By exploring self-expression and vocal empowerment, you'll find that you possess the strength to rise above life's hurdles.

So go ahead—speak up, share your story, and let your voice resonate! Together, as you embrace your unique voice, you'll learn that resilience isn't just a destination; it's a journey filled with creativity, strength, and the will to keep going, no matter what. Your voice is waiting. Are you ready to let it soar?

Chapter Summary

- Create a Voice Empowerment Plan

- Write a letter to yourself about who you want to be

- Embrace your voice and develop resilience

10

EMOTIONAL INTELLIGENCE: THE HEART OF EFFECTIVE LEADERSHIP

Imagine being a leader who not only makes decisions but also truly understands the feelings and needs of their team. That's the magic of emotional intelligence, often called EI. It's like having a special power that helps leaders connect with others, make smarter choices, and achieve great results. In this chapter, we will explore what emotional intelligence is, how it affects leadership, and why it is important for anyone in a position of responsibility—from small business owners to church leaders.

So, what exactly is emotional intelligence? Simply put, it is the ability to recognize, understand, and manage our own emotions while also recognizing and influencing the emotions of others. Unlike IQ, which measures our intellectual abilities, EI is about how we interact with the world around us. Leaders with high emotional intelligence can adapt to various situations, respond to challenges thoughtfully, and create an environment where everyone feels valued and understood.

Think of it this way: a leader with high EI can feel what their team is feeling and respond appropriately. For example, if a team member is feeling stressed about an upcoming project, a leader with strong emotional intelligence will notice their unease and may offer support or lighten their workload. This not only helps the team member but also builds trust and respect—a vital foundation for any successful team.

Research has shown that leaders with high emotional intelligence are often seen as more trustworthy and approachable. This enhances communication within the team, leading to increased collaboration and productivity. Imagine working in a place where you could express your ideas without fear or judgment. That's what emotionally intelligent leaders strive to create—a safe space where everyone's voice matters.

Moreover, emotional intelligence plays a huge role in decision-making. Leaders with high EI are better at balancing logical reasoning with emotional insight. For instance, when faced with a tough choice, these leaders will consider not only the data in front of them but also how their decision will impact their team's morale and overall wellbeing. This kind of thinking leads to better outcomes because it considers the human element in every decision.

Let's take a simple example: a manager deciding whether to implement a new policy. An emotionally intelligent manager would not only look at the facts and figures but also think about how the team feels about the change. They might gather feedback from the team, ensuring that everyone has a say in the process. This not only leads to more informed decisions but also fosters a sense of ownership among team members.

Emotional intelligence also affects how leaders handle conflicts. Conflicts in the workplace can be challenging, but leaders with high EI approach these situations with empathy and understanding. They take the time to listen to all parties involved, recognize emotions, and work towards a solution that satisfies everyone. This approach not only resolves the conflict but can lead to stronger relationships within the team, making it more cohesive and resilient.

It's also important to note that emotional intelligence doesn't mean being overly emotional or letting feelings run wild. Instead, it's about understanding emotions—both your own and those of others—and using that understanding to guide your actions and decisions wisely. A good leader knows when to be firm and when to show compassion.

So, how can you develop your emotional intelligence? The first step is self-awareness. This means taking the time to reflect on your own feelings and understanding how they influence your thoughts and actions. Keeping a journal can be a great way to track your emotions and responses to different situations.

The next step is practice! Engage with your team, ask them about their feelings and opinions, and be open to feedback. This not only helps you grow as a leader but also shows your team that you care. Remember, being approachable and showing empathy can create a positive cycle of communication and trust.

Finally, seek out opportunities for learning. Whether it's through books, workshops, or coaching, investing time in developing your emotional intelligence is a valuable endeavor. The more you know, the better you will become at leading others.

In conclusion, emotional intelligence is the heart of effective leadership. It shapes how leaders manage themselves, relate to others, and make decisions. By understanding and cultivating your EI, you will not only enhance your leadership skills but also create a more engaging and supportive environment for your team. The journey to becoming a leader with high emotional intelligence may take time, but the rewards—stronger relationships, trust, and improved performance—are absolutely worth it. Remember, great leaders aren't just born; they are made through understanding, practice, and a genuine desire to connect with others. Now, it's your turn to embrace the power of emotional intelligence in your leadership journey!

Chapter Summary:

- Recognize emotions in yourself and others to connect better with your team.

- Create a safe space for your team to share ideas without fear of judgment.

- Balance logic and emotions when making decisions to improve team morale.

- Practice self-awareness and seek feedback to enhance your emotional intelligence.

11

DAILY HABITS OF A VOICE-DRIVEN LEADER

Have you ever felt drained after a long day? Perhaps it was because you didn't spend time doing things that truly energized you. It's a tough realization but understanding which habits drain us and which help us thrive can be a game changer in our lives, especially for those of us who want to lead and inspire others. Today, we're going to dive deep into the daily habits of a voice-driven leader and discover how small changes can lead to big transformations.

Habit Drainers: The Sneaky Thieves of Energy

So, what habit drains you? Maybe it's scrolling mindlessly on social media for hours, or perhaps it's listening to gossip that leaves you feeling heavy and uninspired. We often underestimate the impact of negative habits, thinking they don't affect our energy or motivation. But they do! These habits can dim our shine and distract us from our purpose.

Let's take a moment to reflect. Ask yourself, "What is my biggest energy drainer?" Is it the habit of worrying too much about what others think? Or is it striving for perfection in everything you do? Identifying these habits is the first step toward transformation. Once we know what drains us, we can turn our focus to habits that fuel us instead.

The Power of Daily Habits

Every great leader has habits that lift them up. These are the little daily actions that build a strong foundation for success. Imagine waking up every morning and taking just ten minutes to focus on activities that inspire you! That sounds pretty empowering, right? This is where the 10-Minute Routine comes in—a simple yet effective way to jumpstart your day and keep the bad habits at bay.

Here's how it works: take ten minutes each morning to do something that nourishes your soul. You could meditate, reflect on what you're thankful for, or even read a few pages of a book that excites you. This small commitment can create a powerful ripple effect in your life. Think of ten minutes as a tiny investment of time that can yield huge returns!

Embrace Your Gifts

Now, let's connect this to our purpose. As a voice-driven leader, your goal is to help others discover their gifts. How can you do that effectively if you're feeling drained and uninspired? Because, let's be real, how can you shine brightly for others if your own light is flickering? Establishing positive habits is essential for you to energize yourself so that you can do what you love—motivational speaking, teaching, coaching, and inspiring people around you.

When you commit to your 10-Minute Routine, you're not just lifting yourself up; you're setting an example for others. Share your journey! Tell your team about your ten minutes of inspiration. You'll be amazed at how it encourages them to find their own time for reflection and growth.

Setting Boundaries

Another important habit to adopt is learning to set boundaries. It's okay to say no to requests that drain your energy or don't align with your purpose. When your focus is on growth and inspiration, let go of the things that hold you back. Being a voice-driven leader means you are intentional about where you invest your time and energy.

You might find it helpful to think about how you can incorporate these boundaries into your daily routine. Perhaps you could dedicate a certain time to check emails and avoid distractions outside of that. Or limit the time spent with negative people who don't uplift you. Creating these boundaries creates space for more positive habits to flourish!

Celebrate Your Progress

As you begin to develop and embrace new habits, don't forget to celebrate your progress. Every little step counts! Whether it's completing your ten minutes of positive activity or saying no to something that drains you, recognizing these victories is vital. It reminds you of how far you've come on the journey of becoming a better leader.

Keep a journal of your daily wins! Reflect on what works for you and inspire yourself to keep going. Trust me, when you document your progress, it will motivate you to keep those positive habits in place.

Find Your Tribe

Want to amplify your transformation? Surround yourself with other voice-driven leaders! Find a group of people who share your values and are committed to growth. This can be in-person or virtual—but finding your tribe makes a big difference. They can support you on your journey and inspire you to keep up those positive daily habits.

Imagine being part of a community where everyone is cheering each other on! Sharing your struggles and triumphs can lead to motivation that propels you forward. Together, you can create small habits that leave lasting impacts not only on your lives but also on the lives of those you lead.

Putting It All Together

Let's summarize what we've explored. Recognizing the habits that drain our energy is an essential first step for any voice-driven leader. By integrating a daily 10-Minute Routine, we can restore our energy and align ourselves with our purpose. Setting boundaries, celebrating small victories, and finding community support will strengthen these changes.

Remember, small daily habits create transformation. It may not seem significant at first, but when you stick with it, you'll notice big changes over time. You will not only inspire yourself but also inspire others to discover their gifts.

Conclusion: Take Action Tomorrow!

So tomorrow, take a moment to think about one habit you want to let go of and one new habit you will start. Picture yourself as a voice-driven leader stepping into your power, ready to light up the world around you.

Remember, you have the ability to make small changes that can lead to huge transformations—for you and those who look up to you.

Go out there and start your journey; the world is waiting for your unique light!

Chapter Summary:

- Identify your top energy drainer and make a plan to let it go.

- Commit to a 10-Minute Routine each morning to energize your day.

- Set boundaries by saying no to requests that don't support your goals.

- Celebrate small victories to stay motivated on your leadership journey!

12

CRAFTING YOUR PERSONAL VISION STATEMENT: FROM VOICE TO VISION

Welcome to the exciting journey of creating your personal vision statement! You might be asking yourself, "What exactly is a vision statement?" Well, think of it as a treasure map that leads you to your dreams. It's a declaration of your goals and aspirations, a way to see where you want to go, and how to get there. In this chapter, we will walk you through the steps needed to craft a vision statement that truly reflects your values and dreams. So, let's dive in!

What is a Vision Statement?

A vision statement is more than just a fancy sentence. It's like a guiding star in your life's journey. It shows what you hope to achieve in the future and helps you stay on track. Imagine if you were a ship captain navigating the seas. Without a clear destination in mind, you could easily get lost! Your vision statement helps you avoid those rocky waters and keeps you sailing toward your goals.

Step 1: Identify Your Core Values

Before we start writing your vision statement, we need to figure out what really matters to you. This is where your core values come into play. Core values are the beliefs and principles that guide your decisions and actions. To discover them, ask yourself:

- What activities make me feel happy?

- What do I stand for?

- What do I want to contribute to the world?

Taking the time to think about these questions can be eye-opening. For example, if you value honesty, that's likely to influence how you build relationships in business and in life.

Step 2: Set Your Long-Term Goals

Now that you know your core values, it's time for the fun part—setting your long-term goals! Where do you see yourself in five, ten, or even twenty years? Picture your life as if you're imagining a movie. What role do you want to play?

For instance, you might dream of starting a community center that helps children learn, or you might want to strengthen your leadership skills to climb the corporate ladder. The sky's the limit! Jot down all your dreams; don't hold back!

Step 3: Translate Goals into a Vision Statement

Once you've gathered your core values and long-term goals, it's time to craft your vision statement. This should be a vibrant and inspiring sentence that encapsulates all those dreams. Try to keep it concise—one to three sentences is a sweet spot. Think about words that excite you and reflect your journey.

Let's look at an example: "My vision is to create a world where creativity and kindness are at the heart of every community project." See how it combines both aspiration and action?

Examples of Effective Vision Statements

To help you think even more creatively, let's consider some examples from well-known figures.

1. Oprah Winfrey: "To be a teacher and to be known for inspiring my students to be more than they thought they could be."

2. Richard Branson: "To have fun in my journey through life and learn from my mistakes."

Both of these statements are powerful because they reflect personal values and aspirations.

Practical Exercises to Articulate Your Vision

Now that you have some ideas swirling in your head, let's get down to some practical exercises to help you articulate your vision. Grab a piece of paper or open your notes app!

1. Vision Board: Create a collage of images, quotes, and words that resonate with your dreams. This visual representation can serve as a constant reminder of your vision.

2. Write it Down: Take your favorite long-term goal and turn it into a vision statement. Remember to keep it positive and future-focused.

3. Share with a Friend: Talk to a friend or family member about your vision. Sometimes sharing helps clarify your thoughts and gives you valuable feedback!

Revise and Refine Your Statement

After you've created a draft of your vision statement, read it over a few times. Does it resonate with you? If it doesn't spark joy or excitement, tweak it! Keep refining until it feels just right. Your vision statement should inspire you and motivate you to take action.

Putting Your Vision into Action

Now that you have your beautiful vision statement, what do you do with it? It's time to translate that vision into action! Create a plan with short-term goals that lead you closer to your long-term dreams. If your vision is to start a business, break it down into manageable tasks like conducting market research or drafting a business plan.

Celebrate the Small Wins

As you work toward realizing your vision, don't forget to celebrate your milestones. Every step counts! Whether it's completing a task or simply making progress, acknowledging these moments reinforces your commitment to your vision.

Conclusion: Your Journey Begins Here

Remember, understanding and articulating your vision is just the first step toward achieving your goals. It creates a powerful compass that guides you through your journey. By crafting a vision statement that resonates with your core values and long-term dreams, you set the stage for an incredible future. So, get inspired, get writing, and let your vision propel you forward! Your adventures await!

Chapter Summary:

- Identify your core values to understand what truly matters to you.

- Set long-term goals and envision where you want to be in the future.

- Create a concise vision statement that reflects your dreams and aspirations.

- Break down your vision into actionable steps and celebrate your progress!

13

Mentoring: Teach Others How to Lead with Voice

Mentoring is a powerful tool, isn't it? It's not just about sharing your wisdom; it's about creating a future where leaders thrive. If you want to help others blossom into incredible leaders, you need to remember a few key things. So let's jump in and explore how to mentor effectively, helping others find their own voice in leadership.

Building Trust: The Foundation of Mentoring

Before you can teach someone how to lead, you have to build trust. Think of trust like a bridge that connects you and your mentee. Without that sturdy bridge, it's tough to cross over into meaningful conversations. So how do you build trust? Be genuine, honest, and transparent. Share a bit about yourself—not just your successes, but also the bumps in the road. When you show that you're human, your mentee sees the real you, which creates a safe space for them to share their thoughts and insecurities.

The Power of Open Communication

Once trust is established, open communication becomes your best friend. Encourage your mentees to share their ideas and questions without fear of judgment. You might say, "No question is silly!" when a mentee asks something that seems basic. This builds confidence and lets them know that their input is valuable. Remember, communication isn't just talking; it's also about listening. Make sure you're actively listening to their thoughts. Nod, repeat back what they say, and ask follow-up questions. This shows you care and want them to grow.

Setting Expectations Like a Pro

Have you ever tried swimming without knowing the rules? It can get messy! Similarly, when mentoring, setting clear expectations helps everyone stay on track. What do you want your mentees to learn? Discuss goals together and create a roadmap for achieving them. Maybe they want to develop public speaking skills or improve team collaboration. By setting goals, you give your mentees something to aim for—and it helps you measure their progress together.

Active Listening: More Than Just Hearing

Active listening is a biggie in mentoring. It's about tuning in, not just hearing the words your mentee says, but understanding their feelings too. When they share struggles, listen carefully and let them express themselves. Respond with empathy, saying things like, "I can see how that would be difficult." This not only validates their feelings but also opens the door for deeper conversations. When mentees feel heard, they're more likely to take your advice seriously.

Feedback That Fuels Growth

Constructive feedback is the secret sauce to leadership mentoring. Instead of just saying "Good job!" or "That wasn't good!", focus on specific actions. For example, if a mentee did well in a meeting, compliment their preparation and how they encouraged others to participate. If there's room for improvement, frame it positively: "Next time, consider asking for more input from quiet team members; that can really boost creativity!" This kind of feedback not only helps them grow but teaches them how to provide the same feedback to others.

Be a Role Model

People naturally look up to those they admire. So, show your mentees what good leadership looks like by modeling it. Share your experiences, both the highs and the lows. For instance, if you faced a big challenge at work, share how you handled it. Maybe you opened up about your emotions and sought advice from your team. By showing them what leadership means in action, you give them a blueprint to follow.

Celebrate Achievements, Big and Small

Everyone loves a little applause now and then, and your mentees are no different! Take time to celebrate their achievements, whether they're big wins or small victories. Did they lead a successful project for the first time? Throw a mini-celebration. Recognizing their progress boosts their confidence and inspires them to keep pushing forward. Celebrate the journey, not just the destination!

Navigating Challenges Together

Challenges are part of the leadership journey, and you can't just wave a magic wand to make them disappear. But guess what? You can help mentor your mentees through these tricky times. When they hit a roadblock, be right there to guide them. Talk through solutions together, brainstorm alternatives, and help them see it as a learning opportunity. This approach teaches resilience, a key trait of great leaders.

Creating a Cycle of Mentorship

One of the coolest things about mentoring is how it can create a cycle. When you empower your mentees to become leaders, they're more likely to mentor others in return. It's like planting seeds; as each mentored leader blossoms, they can share their knowledge and experiences with others. This push for mentorship within your organization or community creates an enriching environment where leadership flourishes.

Emphasis on Empowerment

At the end of the day, great leadership is not just about directing others; it's about empowering them to take charge themselves. You want your mentees to feel confident in their abilities, making decisions and leading teams. Encourage them to find their voice and speak up. By providing support, guidance, and trust, you create an environment where they can thrive.

Conclusion: The Ripple Effect of Mentorship

In conclusion, remember that mentoring is a chance to multiply leadership. When you mentor effectively, you're not only helping individuals grow, but you're also shaping the future leaders of your organization or community. Your work creates a ripple effect, where each mentee becomes a mentor, and this cycle continues. So, let's get out there, empower others, and watch as leadership blossoms all around us!

Chapter Summary:

- Build trust by sharing your real experiences—successes and struggles alike!

- Encourage open communication and practice active listening with your mentees.

- Set clear goals together to guide mentoring and track progress easily.

- Celebrate all achievements, big and small, to inspire confidence in your mentee!

14

MASTERING YOUR 30, 60, AND 90 DAY ACTION PLAN

Have you ever felt a bit lost when trying to achieve your goals? You're not alone! Lots of people want to become great leaders, but figuring out how to get there can be tricky. That's where a 30, 60, and 90 day action plan comes into play. This plan helps break big goals into smaller, manageable steps. By the end of this chapter, you'll know how to create and implement an action plan that will lead you straight to success!

Why Goals Matter

The first step to getting where you want to go is knowing exactly what that destination looks like. Setting clear and achievable goals is like having a roadmap for your journey. Without goals, it's easy to get sidetracked or lose motivation. Think about it—when you focus on what you want, you're more likely to reach it! So, grab a piece of paper and start brainstorming: what do you want to achieve in 30, 60, and 90 days?

Breaking Down Your Goals

Once you have your goals, it's time to break them down. This is where the magic happens. For each goal, ask yourself what smaller steps you can take. If your goal is to improve your leadership skills, you might break it down into specific tasks, like reading a leadership book, attending a workshop, or seeking feedback from your team. These smaller tasks are much easier to tackle and will keep you moving forward, one step at a time.

The 30-Day Plan

Let's start with the first 30 days. This initial phase is all about learning and starting new habits. Focus on your smaller tasks and make a checklist! Don't forget to set some deadlines. For example, set a goal to finish that leadership book in two weeks. Try to read a little every day, and check it off your list as you go. When you have a checklist, it becomes exciting to see those boxes being ticked off!

The 60-Day Plan

After the first 30 days, it's time to evaluate your progress. What have you learned? What worked well for you? In the next 30 days, build on your successes by adding new tasks and challenges. Maybe you can create an opportunity to practice your new skills by volunteering to lead a small project! This is a great way to put what you've learned into action. Celebrate your progress, no matter how small. Each step is important!

The 90-Day Plan

Now, we're in the home stretch! The last 30 days are your time to reflect and adjust. Look back at what you've accomplished so far. Are there areas where you'd like to improve? Maybe you didn't make as much progress on your goals as you'd hoped. Don't worry; this is a normal part of the process! Adjust your plan as needed. Perhaps you need to change your approach or find new motivation. Keep pressing forward!

Staying Motivated

Throughout this three-month journey, maintaining motivation is key. One great technique is to find an accountability partner. This could be a friend or coworker who understands your goals. You can check in with each other, share progress, and even celebrate when one of you achieves a goal. Sharing your triumphs (and challenges) can make the process much more enjoyable!

Tracking Progress

To maximize your success, tracking your progress is crucial. Create a journal, or use an app to keep tabs on what you're doing. Write down what you accomplished each week. This not only helps you see how far you've come but also provides valuable insights when you're reassessing your goals. And hey, who doesn't love a good reflection at the end of a tough week?

Adjusting Your Plan

Life happens, and sometimes things don't go as planned. Maybe you'll have an unexpected challenge or get sidetracked by other commitments. It's okay! Just because you need to adjust your plan doesn't mean you've failed. In fact, adapting your plan shows that you are a strong leader who can navigate obstacles effectively. Keep your head up and be flexible—fun things can come from rethinking your strategy!

Making Leadership Second Nature

As you work through your 30, 60, and 90-day plan, you'll find that your leadership skills are growing. You're not just checking off tasks anymore; you're learning about yourself and developing new ways to lead others. The more you practice, the more confident you'll become. Remember, it takes time to master something, and that's perfectly okay!

Celebrate Your Successes

At the end of the 90 days, take a moment to celebrate your achievements! Throw a little party for yourself (or a big one if you want)! Reward yourself for your hard work, whether it's a special treat, a fun outing with friends, or simply taking some time to relax. Recognition of your efforts encourages you to keep moving forward on your leadership journey.

The Takeaway

By mastering your 30, 60, and 90-day action plan, you've armed yourself with the skills and strategies needed to achieve your goals systematically. Remember, clear goals, actionable steps, and staying motivated will help you make significant progress. Now that you know how to create a solid plan, go out there and take the first step toward the leader you were always meant to be! The journey may seem daunting at first, but with this structured action plan, you're more equipped than ever to reach your destination. You got this!

Chapter Summary:

- Set clear, achievable goals to create a roadmap for your success journey.

- Break down your big goals into smaller, manageable steps to stay motivated.

- Track your progress and adjust your plan to overcome challenges along the way.

- Celebrate your achievements at the end of 90 days to recognize your hard work!

15

THE IMPORTANCE OF FINDING YOUR AUTHENTIC VOICE

Have you ever wanted to say something important but felt like you couldn't? Maybe it was in a meeting, a class, or even just with friends. Many people struggle with expressing their true thoughts and feelings, and this can be tough! Whether it's due to the pressure of what others think, fears of being judged, or just old experiences that haunt us, finding and using your authentic voice can feel like climbing a mountain. But guess what? It's a journey worth taking!

First, let's think about what authenticity really means. Imagine you're wearing a superhero cape and it feels good. That's you being your true self—the "you" that doesn't hide behind a mask. When you let your authentic self shine, it not only feels liberating but also makes you a stronger leader. Authentic leaders inspire trust and respect because they are real and transparent. People are drawn to those who are genuine, and this can take you far in life and work.

However, expressing your true self doesn't always come easy. Many times, societal expectations push us to act a certain way. Maybe you've felt that you must fit in with your friends or family. This pressure can make you afraid to share your real thoughts or feelings. It's important to recognize these challenges and understand that they are normal. Everyone experiences them at some point!

So, how can we break free from these chains? One of the best tools is self-reflection. This means taking time to think about who you are and what you truly believe. Grab a journal and write down your thoughts or feelings about different situations. Ask yourself questions like, "What do I care about?" or "What makes me happy?" This practice is not just about knowing yourself; it's about understanding your values and passions. The more you know yourself, the easier it will be to express your authentic voice.

Another practical step is to practice communication. It might feel a little uncomfortable at first, but that's okay! Start small. Try sharing your thoughts with someone you trust—a friend or a family member. You could even practice in front of a mirror. This doesn't just help you figure out what to say but also boosts your confidence. Remember, practice makes perfect!

It's also helpful to surround yourself with people who celebrate your authenticity. Look for friends or mentors who encourage you to be yourself, no matter what. These positive relationships will help you feel more secure in sharing your voice. When you are with people who uplift you, it becomes easier to express your thoughts and feelings freely.

We should also consider the impact of authenticity on our relationships. When you speak from the heart, people can feel your honesty. This openness can create stronger bonds and deeper connections with others. Think about it—when was the last time someone shared something real with you? Didn't it feel refreshing? Authentic relationships are built on trust, and sharing your true self is the first step in creating that trust.

Now, let's tie authenticity to leadership. Great leaders are often seen as authentic because they take risks by showing the real them. They don't just follow what everyone else does; they have their own ideas and beliefs. This unique voice can inspire others on their team. When you lead with authenticity, you encourage others to speak out and share their thoughts too. This connection can create a supportive environment where everyone feels valued.

As you venture on this journey of finding your voice, remember that it's okay to stumble a bit along the way. Embracing your authentic self isn't about being perfect, but rather being real. Everyone makes mistakes, and that's part of learning and growing. When you accept this, you'll find it easier to open up and lead from the heart.

So, what's the takeaway here? Finding your voice is essential for personal fulfillment and effective leadership. When you express your true self, you not only benefit personally but also inspire those around you. Whether it's in a friendship, at work, or in your community, authenticity can create ripple effects that lead to positive change.

Keep in mind that embracing your authentic voice is a continuous journey. It takes time, but the rewards are monumental. From increased confidence to stronger relationships, being true to yourself can transform your life. So go ahead! Start your journey today and let your voice be heard. You'll be amazed at how empowering it can be.

Chapter Summary:

- Discover your authentic self by journaling your thoughts and feelings regularly.

- Practice speaking your mind with friends to build communication skills and confidence.

- Surround yourself with supportive people who encourage your true self-expression.

- Embrace mistakes as part of the journey to stronger leadership and personal growth.

16

MEASURING GROWTH: INDICATORS OF LEADERSHIP SUCCESS

Leading a team, whether in a small business, a church, or as a coach, is a journey that demands constant learning and reflection. As a leader, it's essential to think about how you're growing—not just as a person, but also in the eyes of those you lead. Measuring your growth as a leader can feel like a big task, but it can be broken down into manageable parts. Let's explore how to understand your growth and the signs that show you are moving in the right direction.

First of all, it's necessary to recognize that there are two kinds of measurements when evaluating your growth as a leader: internal reflection and external feedback. Internal reflection is all about thinking deeply about your feelings, decisions, and actions. How do you feel about your leadership abilities? Have you made choices you are proud of? On the flip side, external feedback involves looking at how others perceive you as a leader. How does your team feel about your leadership style? What changes do you notice in team morale and motivation? Balancing both perspectives is key to gaining a full picture of your progress.

One of the simplest ways to measure your growth is by looking at five core dimensions of leadership. These dimensions provide a practical framework for understanding where you stand now and what steps you can take to improve. They include Communication, Emotional Intelligence, Team Development, Results Orientation, and Continuous Learning.

Starting with **Communication**, it's essential to assess how effectively you share ideas and information with your team. Think about your conversations. Are you clear, concise, and encouraging? Do you listen to others and provide thoughtful responses? Tools like anonymous surveys can help you gather feedback about your communication skills. If your team feels free to express their ideas, that's a great sign of progress.

Next, let's move on to **Emotional Intelligence**. This means being aware of your feelings and understanding the feelings of others. To measure your growth in this area, reflect on how you handle difficult situations. Are you able to manage stress and respond with empathy? You might keep a journal detailing your feelings during challenging times. An increase in your ability to connect with your team during these moments is a clear indicator of growth.

Team Development is all about how well you nurture your team members. Do you give them opportunities to grow? Conduct regular one-on-one meetings to talk about their dreams and aspirations. If your team members are developing new skills, taking on new responsibilities, and feeling empowered, it shows you're successfully guiding them in their careers.

Then there's the area of **Results Orientation**. This dimension helps you evaluate the effectiveness of your leadership by looking at outcomes. Are you meeting your team's goals? Are there any significant improvements in productivity and efficiency? Set specific goals for your team, and track the progress over time. If you notice significant improvements in performance or the accomplishment of objectives, that's a positive indicator of your growth.

Lastly, **Continuous Learning** is an essential part of being a successful leader. Are you open to new ideas and knowledge? Make it a habit to read books, attend workshops, and seek mentorship. Keep an eye on your development by setting learning goals for the year. If you can list new skills or concepts you have mastered, that's a fantastic sign that you are growing.

These five dimensions—Communication, Emotional Intelligence, Team Development, Results Orientation, and Continuous Learning—create a comprehensive picture of your growth as a leader. They help you focus not only on personal feelings but also on the measurable experiences of your team.

Tracking progress is vital in this journey. Consider creating a leadership growth journal where you can note your reflections and any feedback you've received. By examining changes over time, you can create a clearer picture of how you're evolving as a leader. Celebrate the milestones, no matter how small, as they represent your journey toward success.

In conclusion, measuring your growth as a leader doesn't have to be daunting. By focusing on internal reflection and external feedback, and by using the clear dimensions outlined here, you can create a road map for your leadership journey. Remember, the key takeaway is to be proactive in applying these strategies to track your growth. This isn't just about being a better leader for yourself; it's about being a more effective leader for your team, your business, and your community. Embrace the journey and watch how both you and those you lead flourish!

Chapter Summary:

- Reflect on your feelings and decisions to gauge personal leadership growth.

- Seek feedback from your team to understand their perception of your leadership.

- Foster your team's development through regular one-on-one meetings and opportunities.

- Prioritize continuous learning by reading, attending workshops, and setting learning goals.

17

Resources for Growth

Do you want to be a better leader? Do you dream of inspiring others while also discovering your unique gifts? If your answer is yes, then this chapter is just for you. Leadership is not just about being at the top; it's about nurturing your abilities and learning from the resources available to help you thrive. Let's dive into the world of leadership development, shining a light on the many tools that can help you grow.

One fantastic resource is books. There are countless books written by experienced leaders that offer invaluable wisdom and insights. A classic example is "The 7 Habits of Highly Effective People" by Stephen Covey. Imagine opening a book that encourages you to think differently, empowering you to be proactive, set goals, and build meaningful relationships. These are not just words on a page; they are lessons that can shape your approach to leadership.

Another treasure trove of knowledge is through online courses. Websites like Coursera and Udemy offer courses from renowned experts in leadership. You can learn at your own pace, in your pajamas if you'd like! From understanding emotional intelligence to mastering communication skills, these courses are designed to help you unlock your full potential as a leader.

Picture yourself, with a cup of cocoa in hand, absorbing new ideas that will make you a more impactful leader.

In addition to books and courses, mentorship programs can be a game-changer. Finding a mentor is like having a personal guide who has already walked the path you are on. They can share their experiences, provide advice, and inspire you in ways you might not have imagined. Imagine chatting with someone who believes in you, someone who has faced challenges and can help you overcome your own. That's what mentorship offers—a chance to glean wisdom and encouragement.

Workshops are another exciting avenue for growth. These hands-on sessions allow you to learn in a dynamic environment, surrounded by people who share your interests and passions. You can engage in discussions, participate in role-playing, and tackle real-world problems together. Workshops not only provide knowledge but also build a sense of community. You will walk away not only with skills but also with new friends who are on a similar journey as you.

Resources for Growth: Investing in Your Leadership Development

Let's not forget motivational speaking events! They can change your perspective in ways you never thought possible. When you listen to someone share their journey, it can ignite a fire within you. Inspirational speakers often share stories of overcoming adversity and achieving greatness. Attending these events can fill your heart with hope and your mind with ideas, encouraging you to push forward in your leadership journey.

Podcasts have also revolutionized learning. By merely pressing play on your favorite show, you can absorb hours of valuable leadership content while walking, driving, or even cleaning the house! There are numerous podcasts where leaders interview other leaders, sharing their secrets to success. Imagine filling your ears with powerful stories and strategies that keep you motivated throughout your day.

Networking can be one of the most impactful resources for growth. By connecting with others in your field, you can exchange valuable insights and ideas. Networking events are an opportunity to meet incredible people who can inspire you and extend your knowledge. Who knows? You might meet a future collaborator or discover a new perspective on leadership that transforms your approach.

Let's also highlight online communities for leaders. Websites like LinkedIn and Facebook have groups dedicated to leadership topics. Being part of these communities allows you to share experiences, ask questions, and gain advice from fellow leaders. It's comforting to know that you are not alone on this journey; there are others out there facing similar challenges.

In addition to all these resources, it's essential to consider your own leadership style and how these tools can augment it. Think about what excites you and what areas you want to improve. Do you want to enhance your communication skills? Or maybe improve your emotional intelligence? By identifying your goals, you can tailor your exploration of resources to best suit your needs.

As we wrap up this chapter on leadership development resources, remember: additional resources support growth. Investing in your leadership journey is an ongoing commitment, one that will pay off not only for you but for everyone you lead. The more you learn, the more you can inspire. So take a leap, explore these resources, and watch how they empower you to become the leader you were meant to be!

Your journey toward becoming a successful and inspiring leader begins today. Embrace the resources available to you, and let them guide you in discovering your gifts. The world is waiting for your unique voice—don't keep them waiting any longer! Let's grow together on this path to leadership greatness!Re

18

Key Insights for Impactful Leadership: Three Takaways to Remember

Owning your voice and leading your life is an incredible journey filled with opportunities, challenges, and, most importantly, personal growth. Whether you are a business owner, an entrepreneur, a counselor, a woman leader, or simply someone who yearns for more in life, there is a vibrant world waiting for you. In this chapter, we will dive into three key takeaways that will empower you to take charge of your life and inspire others along the way.

Discovering Your Unique Gifts

First and foremost, the journey begins with discovering your unique gifts. Every person has special talents that make them who they are. Think of those moments when you felt enthusiasm surging through you—when you did something amazing, and it made your heart sing! It could be your ability to solve problems, your knack for making people laugh, or even your talent for leading a team through tough times.

Recognizing these gifts is like finding treasure in your own backyard. To start uncovering them, take some time to reflect. Ask yourself: What do I love doing? What comes naturally to me? Keep a journal and write down the answers. You might be surprised at what you discover! Embrace your gifts, for they are the seeds of your future impact.

The Power of Your Voice

The second takeaway is the unparalleled power of your voice. Your voice is not just about speaking; it's about letting your opinions, passions, and values be heard. Influential leaders know that sharing their thoughts boldly can inspire others to take action.

Picture this: You're in a meeting where everyone seems hesitant to voice their ideas. Suddenly, you share your thoughts, and like magic, others begin to chime in, creating a lively discussion. Your voice ignited a spark of creativity! Remember, your thoughts matter. They can bring change, motivate your team, or foster connections with others. Speak up, for your words hold the power to uplift, encourage, and even transform lives.

Leading with Purpose

Finally, we arrive at the importance of leading with purpose. When you lead with purpose, you set a clear vision of what you want to achieve. It brings a sense of direction to your journey and ignites passion not only within you but in others as well. As a leader, you become a lighthouse, guiding those around you through foggy waters toward a brighter horizon.

Consider a well-known leader like Oprah Winfrey. She didn't just become successful; she led with a purpose to inspire and uplift others. Her mission to connect people and share their stories has created a movement of compassion and understanding. Think about what your own purpose is. What do you want to achieve? How can you inspire others on your journey? When you lead with purpose, people will naturally want to follow.

Time for Action

Now that you've explored these three key takeaways—discovering your unique gifts, harnessing the power of your voice, and leading with purpose—it's time to put this knowledge into action. Each takeaway serves as a stepping stone toward owning your life and achieving impactful leadership.

Imagine the possibilities that await you. When you take charge of your life, you open the door to new experiences, greater success, and meaningful connections. Don't let fear hold you back. Remember, every great leader started from scratch, just like you. Embrace your journey with confidence and enthusiasm.

Embrace Your Inner Leader

In closing, the journey to becoming an impactful leader isn't a straight path; it is filled with twists and turns. But with each step, you will not only learn more about yourself but also inspire others to discover their own gifts. Each person has the potential to make a difference in the world, and it begins with owning your voice and leading with passion.

Take a moment to reflect: What are you waiting for? The world is filled with opportunities for you to shine. It's time to take charge of your life, embrace your unique gifts, speak your truth, and lead with purpose. Go ahead—step boldly into the vibrant future that awaits you! Your journey starts now.

Chapter Summary

- Discover your unique gifts by reflecting on your passions and writing them down.

- Use your voice to inspire and encourage others in every conversation.

- Lead with purpose by setting clear goals and sharing your vision with others.

- Embrace your leadership journey, and confidently tep into your bright future!

19

Conclusion

Embrace Your Power: The Journey Awaits

Congratulations on finishing "Find Your Voice, Lead Your Life!" I'm truly excited for you. This is not just an end—it's the beginning of a powerful journey. Each page of this book has been a stepping stone toward discovering your true potential and embracing the greatness that resides within you.

As you've read, your voice matters. It's a tool you've been given, not just to speak, but to command your narrative and influence those around you. Your value is innate, woven into the very fabric of who you are, and it's time to recognize that! You have something unique to offer, someone who is waiting to be inspired by your journey.

This book has provided you with practical advice, tips, tricks, and countless examples, all designed to help you master the art of self-empowerment. I want you to take a moment and reflect on these key takeaways: Your voice has power, you possess incredible value, and now is the time to embrace the future that you desire.

Sometimes, in the hustle and bustle of being a business owner, an entrepreneur, a coach, a trainer, a teacher, or a ministry leader, we tend to neglect the most important project of our lives: ourselves. We get trapped in a cycle of self-sabotage, thinking we have to play small to fit into the expectations of others. But let me reassure you—it's time to break free from that cycle!

Think about all the lessons you've learned throughout our time together. Whether it was about prioritizing your well-being, setting healthy boundaries, or stepping out of your comfort zone, each lesson is a powerful tool you can wield as you move forward. Remember, every great leader started somewhere, and it wasn't always from a position of strength. It required vulnerability, courage, and an unwavering belief in their own worth.

Now, as you close this chapter of reading, it's critical to move forward armed with the insights you've gained. I encourage you to:

1. Speak up: Start by using your voice—assertively and unapologetically. Share your ideas, your vision, and your passion with those around you.

2. Value Yourself: Remember, you have invaluable contributions to make. Celebrate your achievements, no matter how small, and let them grow into larger victories.

3. Take action: Don't wait for the "perfect" moment to implement what you've learned. There's no perfect moment; there's only now. Let the change begin today!

Your future is shiny and bright, waiting on the other side of your fear and hesitation. I believe in you, and I want you to believe in yourself just as fervently. When you choose to embrace your power and lead with your voice, incredible things happen!

It's time to turn the page from this book to a brand new chapter of your life. Let your journey of self-discovery and leadership inspire not only you but everyone around you. Take the first step today, because it is never too late to become the person you are meant to be.

So, what's stopping you? I urge you, take action now! Whether it's a small step or a giant leap, make it today. Your voice is powerful, your value is undeniable, and your future is waiting for you to claim it!

Let's make your mark on this world together

About the Author

Unlock Your Potential with Dr. Regina Banks-Hall: The Voice of Empowerment

I wrote *Find Your Voice and Live Your Life* because I believe that every individual deserves to uncover their true potential and pursue their passions without hesitation. This book is a heartfelt invitation for you to embrace your unique voice and take bold steps toward achieving the life you've always dreamed of. As a small business owner, female entrepreneur, coach, writer, or manager, you are not just a cog in the wheel; you are the architect of your own destiny, and I am here to guide you on this transformative journey.

With a **Doctorate in Business Administration** and many years of experience as a **Leadership Expert** and **University Dean**, I have honed my skills in empowering others to realize their worth. As a **Small Busi-**

ness Coach** and an **Executive Team Member with** the esteemed **John Maxwell Leadership Organization**, I have had the pleasure of working with countless individuals who have successfully found their voices and pursued their passions. My journey isn't just about titles—it's about understanding the struggles and triumphs that come with building something meaningful. I have faced setbacks and obstacles, just like you. My mission is to share these lessons and inspire you to overcome whatever stands in your way.

This book is your opportunity to spark a change in your life and business. If you're ready to **find your voice**, **ignite your passion**, and embrace the freedom that comes with being your own boss, then dive in. I encourage you to grab your copy of *Find Your Voice and Live Your Life* right now! Let's embark on this exciting journey together and make your biggest dreams a reality. Your voice is powerful—let it be heard!

www.ingramcontent.com/pod-product-compliance
Lightning Source LLC
Chambersburg PA
CBHW050525100526
44581CB00007B/134/J